Action for the Environment

Protecting Habitats

Rufus Bellamy

FRANKLIN WATTS
LONDON • SYDNEY

D0310911

Franklin Watts
96 Leonard Street
London EC2A 4XD

Franklin Watts Australia
45–51 Huntley Street
Alexandria
NSW 2015

ISBN: 0 7496 5535 6

A CIP catalogue record for this book is
available from the British Library

Printed in Malaysia

Editor: Adrian Cole
Design: Proof Books
Art Director: Jonathan Hair
Picture Researcher: Kathy Lockley

Acknowledgements
Pete Atkinson/NHPA 19. Anthony Bannister/NHPA
11 b. Laurie Campbell/NHPA 6, 16 t. James
Carmichael Jr./NHPA 20. © Joyce Choo/CORBIS 14.
Stephen Dalton/NHPA 9 tr, 15 t. DAS Fotoarchiv/Still
Pictures 17. Mark Edwards/Still Pictures Cover b, 25
t. Nick Garbutt/NHPA 29 t, 29 b. © Raymond
Gehman/CORBIS 24. Greenpeace/Morgan 27. David
T. Grewcock/Frank Lane Picture Agency 4 b, 21t.
Martin Harvey/NHPA 13 t. Rich Kirchner/NHPA 5.
John Liddiard/Ecoscene Cover tl, 2, 16 b. © James
Leynse/CORBIS 23. Mark Newman/Frank Lane
Picture Agency 9 b. © Digital VisionLtd, all rights
reserved Cover tr, title page, 18, 28. Fritz Polking
/Still Pictures 4 t. Rex Features 22. Jonathan &
Angela Scott/NHPA 7, 12. Courtesy Soil Association
11 tr. Eric Soder/NHPA 10. Otto Stadler/Still Pictures
25b. Sabine Vielmo/Still Pictures 9 tl. Mike
Whittle/Ecoscene 8. David Woodfall/NHPA 15 b, 21
b. Gunther Ziesler/Still Pictures 26, 31. Daniel
Zupanc/NHPA 13 b

Contents

Habitats are homes

Habitats are the places where animals and plants live. They can be large, like an ocean, or small like a rock pool. They can be home to lots of living things or just a few.

HABITATS ARE IMPORTANT

Habitats are important because they provide animals and plants with food, water and shelter. Many plants and animals can only live in one type of habitat. For example, pandas need bamboo forests to survive. If a habitat is damaged or destroyed then the animals and plants that live there often die. Some habitats, such as forests, also affect the environment in important ways (see pages 8–9).

By protecting habitats, such as bamboo forests in China, we can help save the animals that live there.

HABITATS LOST

For many years people have harmed different habitats. For example, over half of all forests around the world have been destroyed. Road and house building, logging and farming are just some of the causes of this destruction. However, more people now realise that habitats are important and they are helping to restore, care for and protect them.

Hedgerow destruction in Europe. In some countries over 50% of all hedges have been removed, but now people are working to replace them.

Action stations

In New Zealand, landowners have protected large areas of important habitat. Under a scheme called the QEII Trust, they have agreed not to develop or damage specific areas of their land that are important to wildlife. Since the scheme was started, over 60,000 hectares of forests, wetlands, lakes, coastlines and other natural areas have been protected.

The Kaikoura Peninsula in New Zealand is home to many seabirds that would be badly affected if the coastline was damaged by people.

What can be done?

Some habitats, such as mountain areas, have been protected so that people are not allowed to damage them. However, this is not always possible in many places, especially when habitats are close to where people live and work.

PEOPLE PROTECTING NATURE

Where people live alongside nature, many things can be done to look after the environment. Anti-pollution laws help to protect many habitats, such as rivers and lakes. House and road building can be controlled to limit the effect on the surrounding habitat. Farmers are encouraged to conserve habitats, such as wetlands, instead of destroying them.

This heather moor is in northern England. Habitats like this are often threatened by human development.

HELPING HABITATS SURVIVE

Some habitats, such as heather moors, have been partly created by people. These also need to be looked after so that the wildlife they support can survive. Many habitats recover naturally if they are damaged but many of the animals and plants that once lived there may already be dead.

These wildebeest in Kenya travel across huge distances in search of food. Without the safety of a large, protected reserve, people could move on to the land and the number of wildebeest would fall.

Action stations

For successful habitat protection, enough land must be protected to give animals and plants the space they need to live, feed and breed. Protecting only a small area of a habitat often does not work. In Africa, countries are working together to set up cross-border protected areas. These will be large enough to let animals migrate many hundreds of kilometres in search of food, water and breeding grounds.

Forests forever

Forests and woods are very important habitats and are home to about half of all types of animals and plants. They affect the weather and help to keep the Earth at the right temperature, and also stop soil washing away. Despite this, an area of forest about the size of 40 football pitches is being destroyed every minute.

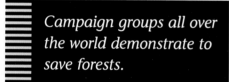
Campaign groups all over the world demonstrate to save forests.

FOREST CAMPAIGNS

The world's oldest forests are home to an especially large number of animals and plants. Some of them, like the Taman Negara Forest in Malaysia, are protected by law. Campaign groups are pressing for many more areas of 'old growth' forest to get protection, and for governments to stop illegal logging and other types of forest destruction.

PLANTING THE FUTURE

A lot can also be done to help look after and restore forests. Some forestry companies now plant many saplings for every tree they cut down. Well-managed forests are checked by international organisations, such as the Forest Stewardship Council. Wood from these forests is given a special label (see above).

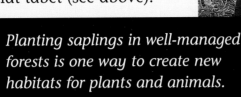

Planting saplings in well-managed forests is one way to create new habitats for plants and animals.

Action stations

Many millions of people live in forests. In countries such as Ecuador in South America, the WWF and other organisations are working with local communities to help them protect, conserve and make a living from their forest homes. These communities harvest wood and other resources in ways that do little harm to the forest. They can then sell these things to make money.

This banana farmer from Ecuador can help to protect the land he works on.

Farmers in action

Farming has damaged many habitats around the world. For example, prairies in the USA and Canada that were once home to buffalo are now occupied by farms, which mainly grow crops such as wheat.

WILDLIFE-FRIENDLY FARMING

An increasing number of farmers, in places such as Europe, Canada and the USA, are now trying to reduce the amount of damage their work does. They are replanting habitats such as woods and hedges and are using fewer or no artificial chemicals to feed and protect their crops (see right).

Farmers can create new habitats, like this strip of wild flowers, simply by leaving an area of crop-free land around their fields.

Action stations

In many countries, some farmers now grow food using organic methods. They do not use artificial chemicals to feed crops. Instead, organic farmers use animal manure and other natural products. This reduces the pollution of local rivers, streams and other habitats. Organic fields can also support a wider variety of wildlife. Many people buy organic food because it benefits the environment and because they think it is healthier and tastes better than non-organically farmed food.

The Soil Association Organic Standard labels food so people know it has been organically grown.

TREES NOT DESERTS

In places such as Africa, farming has turned many habitats into desert, partly because of overgrazing by cattle. To stop this happening many farmers are now growing plants that protect the soil and provide a habitat for wildlife. For example, women farmers from the Greenbelt Movement in Kenya have planted millions of trees over the last few decades to stop soil erosion.

This land in Namibia, Africa has been turned into desert by farming and overgrazing.

Habitats and holidays

One of the most famous habitats in the world is the African savannah – the home of lions, elephants and other 'big game'. Large areas of this habitat, such as the Masai Mara national reserve in Kenya, are protected areas.

PROTECTING NATURE

Tourists visiting African wildlife reserves spend millions of pounds a year. This money not only helps pay for habitat protection, but also provides a strong reason for African countries to look after their wild areas. Tourism benefits many other places in a similar way – from the rainforests of Malaysia to Australia's Great Barrier Reef.

Lions and other big game attract tourists from all over the world. Tourism brings much-needed money to help conservation in many developing countries.

TOURISM IMPACT

Unfortunately tourism can also harm the environment. For example, tourist vehicles disturb animals and crush plants. Eco-tourism holidays are designed to reduce this environmental impact to a minimum. Organisations such as the WWF also work to make sure that tourism benefits local people – so they have a reason to help conserve the wild areas where they live.

These eco-tourists are in the Danum Valley rainforest in Malaysia. The walkway stops them disturbing the environment.

Action stations

The Warrawong Earth Sanctuary in the Adelaide Hills, Australia, is a protected area that contains some unique habitats. These are home to amazing animals such as Brown Bandicoots and Tammar Wallabies. The tourists who visit the sanctuary help pay to protect it. Warrawong is just one of many Earth Sanctuaries across Australia.

People visit Earth Sanctuaries to see animals, such as this Tammar Wallaby, in their natural habitat.

Protecting the urban jungle

Gardens, parks and even wasteground provide important habitats for plants and animals in cities and towns. The 'green space' around some urban areas is disappearing under new roads and buildings. However, some cities and towns are creating new green space to bring more wildlife into people's lives.

PARKS AND FORESTS

Parks in many cities are being managed to attract wildlife. For example, in Singapore, areas of grass are kept long to create a habitat for birds. New wildlife areas are also being created around other cities. For example, in the UK, 12 large community forests are being planted. Most of this woodland is on wasteground on the edge of urban areas.

Playing in a park in Singapore. The authorities in Singapore attract both people and wildlife to the city's parks by careful habitat management, which includes collecting litter.

GREEN CORRIDORS

Habitats can also be created in cities along the edges of roads, rivers and railways. These 'green corridors' are being created in countries, such as Australia and Canada, to link green spaces together and to bring a bit of the countryside into the town.

Some cities are home to an amazing variety of animals, including foxes.

Action stations

In many cities private gardens are a vital habitat, especially for birds. If you have a garden you can make it a better habitat by planting flowers, such as buddleias, and by putting up 'bug boxes'. Both of these will attract insects. Also, put out water and bird food to encourage birds to share your garden.

Even if you do not have a garden at home, you may be able to create a wildlife habitat elsewhere. This nature garden is at a school.

Coastal conservation

Coastlines are important habitats for wildlife; they also often protect the land in-shore from damage by wind and waves.

MANGROVE FORESTS AND MARRAM

Protecting coastal plants is vital. For example, mangrove forests stop land erosion and give fish a place to breed. Despite this, many are threatened. In recent years, conservation groups have worked hard to get them protected. Sand dunes protect coastlines from flooding. In places like Scotland, volunteers plant marram grass to stop dunes eroding.

The roots of marram grass help to hold sand dunes together.

REEF WATCH

Coral reefs are found in warm coastal waters. They are home to about a quarter of all the species that live in the sea. Unfortunately, about 80% of reefs are in danger of becoming polluted or destroyed by changing sea temperatures. The Great Barrier Reef in Australia is the largest in the world. Plans to save it include reducing coastal pollution and enlarging the protected areas of the reef.

The activity of tourists on the Great Barrier Reef is strictly controlled, so that they do not damage the delicate coral.

Action stations

Pollution is a big problem in many habitats because it makes them unsafe for animals and plants. This is a particular problem along coastlines. Rubbish, for example, can choke fish, sea birds and other creatures. To do something about this problem, hundreds of thousands of people in about 100 countries around the world take part in the annual International Coastal Clean-up. Each year thousands of tons of rubbish are picked up.

These volunteers are cleaning up after an oil spill – one of the more serious forms of habitat pollution.

Saving the seas

The world's seas and oceans are home to a vast number of living things, but they have been badly polluted in the past by everything from oil spills to sewage. New laws are being passed to try to protect the seas.

PROTECTING FISH

Modern fishing fleets catch so many fish that some species, including those that were once common such as cod, are becoming scarce. This 'overfishing' can affect the whole ocean habitat because it upsets the balance of creatures in the 'food chain'. Action is now being taken to increase fish numbers. For example, the European Union has agreed to reduce the amount of fishing it carries out.

Seas cover over 70% of the Earth's surface. Water pollution can poison fish and destroy a variety of habitats.

CLEANER SEAS

Public pressure has meant that there is increasing action to clean polluted seas. As a result a lot of human sewage and industrial waste that was once dumped straight into the sea is now fully cleaned in treatment plants. Laws have been passed in places like Europe and the USA to stop oil being carried by old ships, which can be easily damaged.

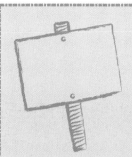

Action stations

Many seas around the world are polluted with chemicals called phosphates and nitrates. These come from products such as washing detergents and farm fertilisers. They cause large toxic 'blooms' of tiny plants called algae. Campaign groups in many countries have persuaded people to do something about this problem. For example, to help the highly-polluted Baltic Sea, many people in Sweden use phosphate-free washing detergents.

Algal blooms like this one can be reduced if people buy 'low phosphate' detergents.

Wet and wild lands

Wetlands are damp and watery places such as swamps, fens, marshes and bogs. They are very important habitats, especially for birds. Many wetlands have been drained and turned into farmland. However, more is now being done to protect these sites.

RESTORING WETLANDS

Many wetlands that were drained are being flooded again. In the USA an important project has begun to solve the problems facing the Florida Everglades. These massive wetlands have been badly damaged because developments, such as flood defences and farming, have reduced the supply of the water they depend on. New plans – that will cost billions of dollars – aim to restore the water supply.

Flood defences and farming have lowered the level of water in the Everglades and threaten to change the habitat forever.

CLEANING THE WATER

Wetlands are often polluted with farm chemicals and sewage. However, these problems can be solved. For example, in the Norfolk Broads in the UK, pollution from sewage works is cleaned up before it gets into this area of marsh, fens, rivers and lakes. Polluted mud is also removed using giant riverbed 'vacuum' cleaners.

Pollution control stops wetland habitats becoming damaged – so that people and animals can enjoy the lakes and rivers.

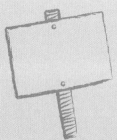

Action stations

Peat bogs are formed by decaying plants, such as sphagnum moss. Many bogs have been mined for peat – which is used in gardens – and destroyed. Recently, some companies have stopped selling peat because of pressure from campaigners and the public. Key peat bogs have been protected and peat cutting is being stopped.

People who buy peat-free compost help to stop the destruction of peat bogs.

Rivers of life

Pollution from sewage works, factories and farming has meant that many rivers around the world are polluted. Some, like the Ganges in India, are so dirty that they are a threat to human health.

RIVER CLEAN-UP

Some river and lake habitats have been made much cleaner in recent years. Fish have returned to rivers such as the Rhine in Germany, which were heavily polluted. This is thanks to laws that limit the amount of waste that can be disposed of in rivers and lakes.

SAVE WATER

Rivers and lakes face many other problems. One of the most serious is the overuse of water. For example, the Aral Sea in Central Asia has shrunk by over 50% because river water has been used to grow cotton. In many countries, people are often asked to limit their water use during hot, dry weather to prevent water shortages.

These boats are trapped in sand in what was the Aral Sea – once the world's fourth largest lake. Areas of this watery habitat have been turned into sand dunes because too much water was taken for irrigation.

Action stations

Large dams provide electricity and water for irrigation and drinking; however, they also cause many habitats — especially those along river banks — to be flooded and destroyed. Today, many people question whether large dams should be built. For example, in India, village people have campaigned against the damming of the Narmada Valley. In some countries, the tide is changing. In the USA some dams are now being taken down.

This dam on the Kennebec River, Maine, USA, was taken down to restore fish and bird habitats.

Protecting the peaks

Mountain habitats are some of the most beautiful in the world. They are home to many rare animals and plants, and are also the places where rivers start. Protecting these habitats helps to keep rivers flowing properly.

A forest fire at Yellowstone National Park. Tourists can cause serious problems for certain habitats.

MOUNTAIN PARKS

Many mountain and upland areas are protected. In fact, the high country of the Yellowstone National Park in the USA was the first area in the world to be made a national park. However, many popular mountain areas are suffering from problems, such as footpath erosion, created by too many tourists.

SAVING TREES

Erosion is also a problem in many mountain areas. For example, in Nepal, soil is washed away because trees are destroyed by logging and overgrazing. People also use wood for fuel. To stop this, local people are planting new trees, controlling and changing farming and using new types of stove which burn less fuel.

In Nepal, tree planting is helping to stop mountain soil from being washed away.

Action stations

The Alps are one of the most important mountain areas in Europe. However, they face many problems including air and water pollution, deforestation and pressures caused by tourism. Many groups are working to protect the fragile Alpine habitats. For example, a group called Alp Action has planted more than half a million trees in six Alpine countries. Mountain forests help protect natural habitats from problems such as flooding and erosion.

The mountain habitats of the Alps, home to many animals and plants, are threatened by human activity.

25

Protecting the poles

The Arctic and Antarctic, and the seas around them, are the world's largest wilderness habitats. They are home to animals including polar bears and penguins. Protecting the two polar regions is of the greatest importance because they are still so unspoilt.

PROTECTED CONTINENT

Thanks to the Antarctic Treaty, Antarctica is the first continent in the world to be made a conservation area. This treaty protects the region – which covers about 10% of the Earth's surface – in many ways. For example, the treaty bans mining for a minimum of 50 years.

Despite the freezing temperatures, the poles are home to a variety of wildlife, including these penguins in Antarctica.

ARCTIC ACTION

Although many areas of the Arctic are protected, some are still threatened by overfishing and oil exploration. Campaign groups, such as Greenpeace, work tirelessly to stop this happening and to prevent tourism and other industries damaging the region.

Greenpeace activists monitor the Antarctic Ocean. Their work helped to secure the Antarctic Treaty.

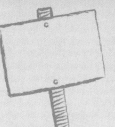

Action stations

Greenpeace is one environmental campaign group that monitors Antarctica for damage, such as that caused by tourism and fishing. However, the destruction of the fragile polar habitats by global warming is an even greater threat and can only be solved with the help of people in all countries (see page 28).

The future

In the next decade and beyond, habitat protection will become even more important as pressures on the natural world increase and new cities, roads and other developments threaten the countryside.

Trees take in carbon dioxide and release it when they are burnt. Forest protection is therefore vital in the fight against global warming.

GLOBAL WARMING

One of the biggest threats to habitats in the future comes from global warming. This is thought to be happening because human activity has made levels of 'greenhouse' gases, such as carbon dioxide, rise beyond 'natural' levels. These gases act like the panes of glass in a greenhouse and are causing the Earth to warm up.

HABITATS IN DANGER

Many habitats will be threatened if temperatures rise by even a few degrees Celsius. Animals and plants could be killed or will have to move as temperatures increase. Coastal habitats will be in particular danger because sea levels will rise as the ice at the poles melts. Over 100 countries have agreed to work together to combat global warming; however, it may already be too late to stop it having some effect on habitats in years to come.

Action stations

Habitat conservation is a challenge for every country and person in the world. However, some scientists have highlighted the habitats that they think are the most important ones to save. These 25 conservation 'hotspots' are the places that contain the richest variety of animals and plants and are the most threatened. They include the island of Madagascar (see page 31).

Island habitats, like that of Madagascar, are among the most threatened by global warming. Animals there, including Giant Day Geckos and Ring-tailed Lemurs, could disappear if temperatures rise.

Glossary

Bug box A special container designed to give insects a place to live and breed.

Carbon dioxide A gas produced when fossil fuels, such as petrol, are burned. It is one of the major 'greenhouse' gases.

Coral reef An underwater habitat found in warm, shallow coastal seas. Reefs are mainly made up of the skeletons of corals.

Deforestation The clearing of trees for farmland or other development.

Developed world The wealthier countries of the world, in which there are highly developed industries.

Developing world The poorer countries in the world, which rely more on farming than on industry.

Eco-tourism A type of tourism designed to have little impact on the environment.

Erosion The gradual wearing away of rock and soil by things such as wind, waves and rain.

Fertilisers Substances added to soil to make plants grow faster or bigger. Fertilisers can be natural or man-made.

Food chain The eating order in nature, usually starting with plants and ending with meat-eating animals.

Global warming The increase in global temperatures that is thought to be occurring due to the effect of 'greenhouse' gases in the Earth's atmosphere.

Green corridor A long strip of vegetation, normally along a river, road or railway, that allows animals to move between larger natural areas.

Greenhouse gases Gases such as carbon dioxide that are produced by burning fossil fuels. These gases trap heat in the atmosphere, so that it cannot escape into space.

Green space An area, such as a park in a city or town, which has not been built on and has grass and other vegetation including trees.

Habitat The place where an animal or plant lives, breeds and gets the food and water it needs.

Irrigation The watering of land for growing crops.

Mangrove A type of plant with stilt-like roots that grows along coasts in the tropics.

Marram A type of grass that grows along sandy shores and is planted to hold sand dunes together.

Nitrate A chemical that is used as, among other things, a fertiliser to help plants grow.

Organic farming A way of farming that does not use any man-made fertilisers or other man-made agricultural chemicals.

Peat bogs Types of habitat mainly formed from the partly decomposed remains of plants.

Phosphate A chemical that is used as, among other things, a fertiliser to help plants grow.

WWF One of the world's most important conservation organisations that campaigns to save endangered species and their habitats.

Find out more

These are Conservation International's 25 habitat hotspots. Search the Internet to find out more about each one, or log on to the website below.

North and Central America
Caribbean
California Floristic Province
Mesoamerica

South America
Tropical Andes
Choco-Darien (Western Ecuador)
Atlantic Forest
Brazilian Cerrado
Central Chile

Europe and Central Asia
Caucasus
Mediterranean Basin

Africa
Madagascar and Indian Ocean Islands
Eastern Arc Mountains and Coastal Forests
Guinean Forests of West Africa
Cape Floristic Region
Succulent Karoo

Mainland Asia
Mountains of Southwest China
Indo-Burma
Western Ghats

Asia–Pacific
Philippines
Sundaland
Wallacea
Southwest Australia
New Zealand
New Caledonia
Polynesia and Micronesia

www.biodiversityhotspots.org
The hotspot website from Conservation International contains a wealth of useful material, including information about conservation action, human impact on the environment and different habitats.

Index